Alien at the Zoo

Story by Brian and Jillian Cutting

2

"Look at that pouch!
What animal is that?"

"That's a kangaroo."

"Look at that neck!
What animal is that?"

"That's a giraffe."

6

"Look at that stomach! What animal is that?"

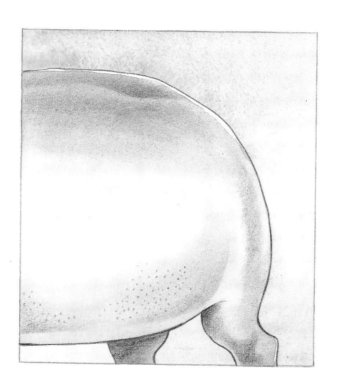

"That's a hippopotamus."

"Look at that mouth!
What animal is that?"

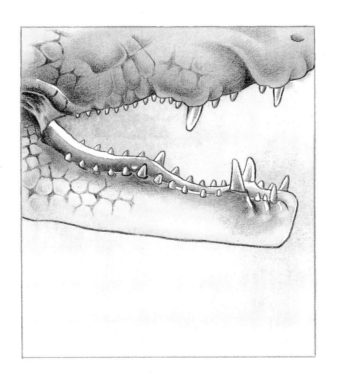

"That's a crocodile."

10

"Look at that tail!
What animal is that?"

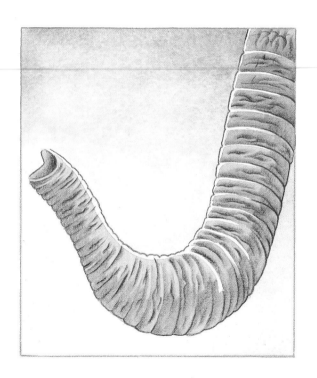

"That's not a tail.
That's a trunk.
That's an elephant."

12

"Look at that paw!
What animal is that?"

"That's a lion."

"I like your zoo,"
said the alien.

"Come and see **my** zoo."